TOP 50 QUESTIONS

Wild Earth

SEYMOUR SIMON

SCHOLASTIC INC.

New York Toronto London Auckland Sydney
Mexico City New Delhi Hong Kong Buenos Aires

To my sister Miriam with love from her younger brother (despite what she says)

Acknowledgments

Special thanks to my wonderful and super-fast editor, Jenne Abramowitz. Thanks also to Kevin Callahan for his lively, eye-catching design and to Karen Brooks and Elizabeth Van Houten for their very skillful copyediting. The author is deeply grateful to David Reuther for his editorial and design suggestions, as well as his enthusiasm for this project. Also, many thanks to Gina Shaw at Scholastic Inc. for her extraordinary support through the publication of the "Top 50 Questions" series.

Photo Credits

Front cover and page 18: © Jim Sugar/Corbis; back cover and pages 4, 7 (both), 11, 15 and 20: © Gary Hincks/Photo Researchers, Inc.; page 1: © Imelda Medina/epa/Corbis; page 3: © Christian Darkin/Photo Researchers, Inc.; page 5: © SPL/Photo Researchers, Inc.; page 6: © David R. Frazier Photolibrary, Inc./Photo Researchers, Inc.; page 8: © Daniel Sambraus/ Photo Researchers, Inc.; page 9: © Kevin Callahan/Scholastic; page 10: © D. Parker/Photo Researchers, Inc.; pages 12 and 27: © United States Geological Survey; page 13: © TWPhoto/Corbis; page 16: © Martin Rietze/Getty Images; page 17 (top): © Francesco Ruggeri/Getty Images.; page 17 (bottom): © Paul A. Souders/Corbis; page 18: © Jim Sugar/Corbis; page 19 (top): © George Steinmetz/Corbis; page 19 (bottom): © Stephen & Donna O'Meara/Photo Researchers, Inc.; page 21 (top): © Bruce Molina/Terra Photographics/Earth Science World Image Bank; page 21 (bottom): © imagebroker/Alamy; page 22: © Hoa-Qui/Photo Researchers, Inc.; page 23: © Chuck Babbit/iStockphoto; page 24: © Sally Bansusen/Photo Researchers, Inc.; page 25: © Paula Bronstein/Corbis; page 29: © Galen Rowell/Corbis; page 30: © Arno Balzarini/epa/Corbis; page 31: © Anatoly Maltsev/epa/Corbis.

ISBN-13: 978-0-439-79601-9
ISBN-10: 0-439-79601-6

Copyright © 2009 by Seymour Simon

12 11 10 9 8 7 6 5 4 3 2 1   9 10 11 12 13 14/0

Printed in the U.S.A.
First printing, January 2009

① What is the earth's crust?

The earth has three main layers: the crust, the mantle, and the core. The crust is the outer layer or "skin" of the earth. It's about 20 to 35 miles thick under land and 4 to 7 miles thick under the oceans. If you compared the size of the earth with an apple, the crust would be thinner than the apple's peel.

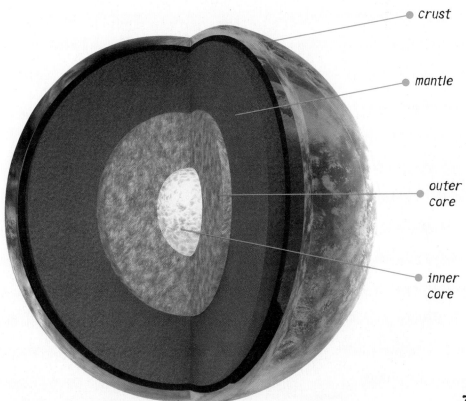

crust

mantle

outer
core

inner
core

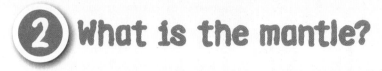

② What is the mantle?

The mantle is a layer of hot, heavy rock that lies under the crust. It stretches 1,800 miles deep into the earth. The upper part of the mantle moves in slow motion.

③ What's at the earth's core?

The outer core lies beneath the mantle and is about 1,350 miles deep. The outer core is very hot and is thought to be made of mostly molten iron and nickel. The inner core reaches down another 750 miles to the center of the earth. The inner core is very hot—about 13,000° Fahrenheit (about 7,200° Celsius). That's hotter than the surface of the sun.

④ What are plates?

The earth's crust is broken up into huge sections like a cracked eggshell. These plates drift very slowly on top of the mantle.

⑤ What happens when plates move?

Plates can move from side to side. They can also move up and down. Most move at just a fraction of an inch per year. Most of the earth's volcanoes and earthquakes occur at the boundaries between plates as they scrape together or move away from each other. The theory of plate movement and its effects is called plate tectonics.

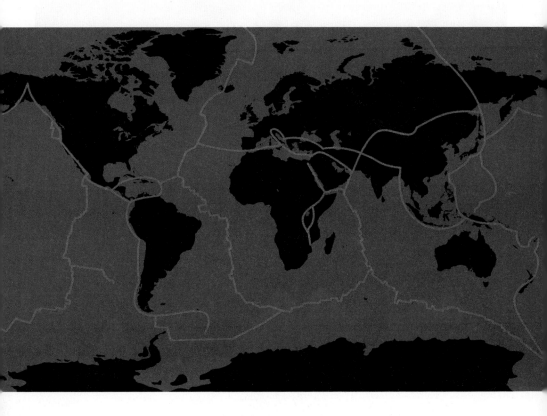

6 How do mountains form?

Mountains may form when two plates push against each other. The land at the edges of the plates lifts and folds over itself.

7 What causes an earthquake?

Most earthquakes are caused by a sudden, violent shift of the earth's plates. Rocks at the edge of the plates break underground. The motion spreads out from the break in waves like the ripples in a pond when a stone is dropped. Large earthquakes can be very destructive.

8 Where does an earthquake occur?

The point on the surface where an earthquake occurs is called the epicenter. But the actual place where most earthquakes start is usually a few miles below the epicenter. This is called the focus of the quake.

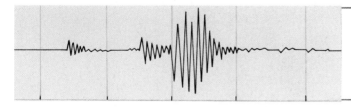

We learn about the size and location of earthquakes using an instrument called a seismometer.

9 What is an aftershock?

An aftershock is a smaller earthquake that follows a major earthquake. Big earthquakes can have many aftershocks. Sometimes an aftershock can happen weeks or months after an earthquake.

10 What is a fault?

Faults are deep cracks in the earth's crust where two blocks of rock meet. Faults can range in length from less than an inch to thousands of miles. Faults allow the blocks to move. The rocks on one side of a fault slip against the other side during an earthquake.

⑪ Are there different kinds of faults?

Faults are grouped by the angle and the direction of the movement of the two sides of the fault.

Dip–Slip Fault

When one side of the fault drops downward, it's called a dip-slip fault.

When one side moves up and over the other side of the fault, it's called a thrust fault.

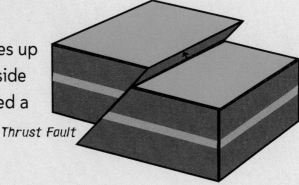

Thrust Fault

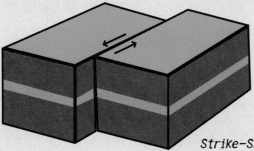

When rocks move horizontally along the surface, it's called a strike-slip fault.

Strike–Slip Fault

⑫ Where is the San Andreas Fault?

The San Andreas Fault runs for 800 miles through western and southern California and Baja California in Mexico. The San Andreas Fault was the site of the devastating 1906 San Francisco earthquake, in which more than 3,000 people died.

⑬ How long do earthquakes last?

Small earthquakes last for a second or two. Larger ones can shake for a minute or more.

14 How often do earthquakes happen?

There are about a million earthquakes in the world each year. Most of them are too small to notice. About 100,000 earthquakes are big enough to be felt and about 100 of these cause some damage. Major earthquakes happen about once a year.

15 Which region has the most earthquakes?

About 75 percent of the world's earthquakes happen along the edge of the Pacific Ocean, from the west coasts of South, Central, and North America, to Japan, China, the Philippines, and Indonesia. Alaska and California have the most earthquakes of any state in the U.S.; Florida and North Dakota have the fewest.

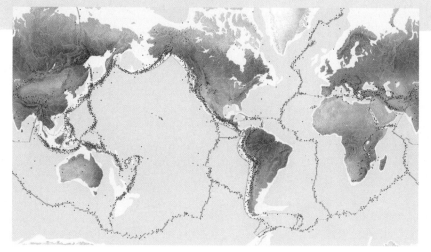

16 What is the Richter scale?

The Richter scale measures the amount of energy an earthquake releases, and therefore how powerful it is. Each number on the Richter scale stands for an earthquake 10 times more powerful than the number below it. For example, a magnitude 2 earthquake is hardly noticeable. But a magnitude 3 earthquake is ten times stronger and more easily felt. Every earthquake above magnitude 6 causes a lot of damage.

17 Which was the most powerful earthquake in the United States?

A magnitude 9.2 earthquake struck Prince William Sound, Alaska, on Good Friday, March 27, 1964.

18 Which was the most powerful quake in the world?

A magnitude 9.5 earthquake struck Chile on May 22, 1960. More than 2,000 people died and 2 million were left homeless.

19 Why are major earthquakes so dangerous?

Big earthquakes are dangerous because they cause buildings, bridges, and highways to collapse. They may cause fires by breaking gas mains. Some earthquakes trigger landslides and giant sea waves called tsunamis.

(20) Can you prepare for an earthquake?

If you live in an area where earthquakes are common, you and your family should have disaster supplies on hand such as flashlights, bottled water, canned food, and first aid kits. You should talk about what to do and where to go in your home before an earthquake happens.

(21) What should you do if you're in an earthquake?

If you are inside a building, get under a table. Protect your head with a cushion or a towel. Leave the building as soon as possible if you smell gas. Always use the stairs to leave, not the elevators. If you are outside, stay away from buildings and electrical wires. Aftershocks can cause more damage, so make sure to ask an adult if it's safe to go back inside.

VOLCANOES

22 How does a volcano form?

Like mountains, volcanoes form when plates collide.
Sometimes, one plate pushes over the top of another plate.
As the bottom plate slides downward into the mantle,
it begins to melt. There is a great deal of pressure in
the mantle. A volcano is a kind of giant safety valve that
releases pressure. A volcano
erupts when melted,
or molten, rock pushes
up through
cracks in the
crust.

23 What comes out of a volcano?

Molten rock, pieces of solid rock, cinders, and ash are expelled when a volcano erupts. The rock, cinders, and ash pile up around the volcano. The pile grows larger and larger until the mountain is shaped like a cone.

24 What is magma?

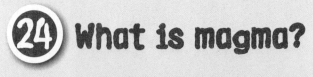

Hot, melted rock within the earth is called magma.

25 What is lava?

Magma that comes to the earth's surface is called lava. Lava is liquid rock that ranges from 1,300° to 2,200° Fahrenheit (1,200° Celsius). That's up to ten times hotter than boiling water.

26 Are there different kinds of lava?

There are two main kinds of lava. Both have Hawaiian names. *Aa* (AH-ah) is thick and slow-moving. It hardens into a rough tangle of broken, sharp rocks when it cools. *Pahoehoe* (pah-HOH-ey-hoh-ey) is thin and flows quickly. Pahoehoe flows down the slopes of a volcano faster than a person can run. It forms a smooth, billowy surface when it hardens.

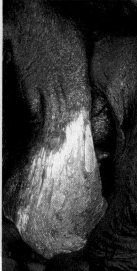

Pahoehoe

27 Are there different kinds of volcanoes?

There are three main types of volcanoes. Shield volcanoes have broad, gentle slopes like a warrior's shield. They have histories of quiet lava flows. Cinder cone volcanoes look like piles of rough rock and sand, with steep sides and large craters. They erupt repeatedly and explosively. Composite volcanoes have both violent explosions and quieter lava flows.

28 What happens to volcanic cinders and ash?

Volcanic cinders and ash are blown high in the sky during a volcanic eruption. Most of the time they settle down around the mouth of the volcano and form a cinder cone mountain. But sometimes the cinders and ash are swept far away by winds. A gigantic volcanic explosion can cause spectacular sunsets and colder winters around the world for the next several years.

29 What are volcanic blocks and bombs?

Volcanic blocks are solid pieces of rock, some many feet across, which are flung into the air by a volcanic eruption. Volcanic bombs are smaller, hot lava rocks that become rounded in shape as they fly through the air. Volcanic blocks and bombs can be hurled as far as 10 miles and cause much damage when they fall.

Volcanic bomb

③⓪ What is the Ring of Fire?

The Pacific Ring of Fire is a 25,000-mile-long band of earthquake-prone areas and volcanoes that encircles the Pacific Ocean. It is home to about 450 active and dormant volcanoes.

③① Which country has the most volcanoes?

Indonesia has over 130 active volcanoes, more than any other country. The majority of these volcanoes are on Indonesia's two largest islands: Java and Sumatra.

Mount St. Helens in Washington state

32 Are there active volcanoes in the United States?

About 50 volcanoes have erupted in the United States in the last 200 years. About 40 of those volcanoes are in Alaska's Aleutian Island chain. There are one or two sizable eruptions from an American volcano each year.

33 What kinds of rocks are formed by volcanoes?

Rocks formed by volcanoes are called igneous or fire-formed rocks. The speed at which the lava cools and the minerals in the lava determine the kind of rock that's formed. Basalt and obsidian are common forms of volcanic rocks.

Obsidian

(34) Can we predict volcanic eruptions?

It is very difficult to predict the exact time a volcano will erupt. However, volcanoes often erupt after magma swells up under a volcano's slopes. Scientists set up monitoring devices to measure these swells of magma in volcanoes that are near populated areas so they can warn people of a coming eruption.

(35) Do any good things come from volcanoes?

Volcanoes create new mountains, new islands, and soils rich in minerals. Plants soon grow in the cracks in volcanic rock after an eruption, and animals return to eat them. The fiery explosion of a volcano is a sign of the rebirth of an ecosystem.

36 What is a tsunami?

A tsunami is a giant sea wave, sometimes called a tidal wave. But tsunamis have nothing to do with tides. Tsunamis are caused by the motion created by earthquakes or volcanic eruptions in or near the oceans.

37 How big do tsunamis get?

Tsunamis are usually less than 3 feet high in deep water. But the wave height can reach over 100 feet as tsunamis travel into shallow water.

38 How fast do tsunamis move?

The speed of a tsunami depends upon the depth of the water through which it's traveling. Tsunamis travel about 40 miles per hour in 100 feet of water. But tsunamis travel at speeds of 450 to 600 miles per hour in the open ocean at depths of 14,000 feet or greater.

39 How far can tsunamis travel?

Tsunamis can travel great distances. For example, the Great 1960 Chilean tsunami was generated by a 9.5 magnitude earthquake in Chile. The quake caused enormous waves thousands of miles away in Hawaii and Japan.

Earthquake
focus

40 What kind of damage does a tsunami do?

Buildings, docks, and bridges break and are destroyed when a giant tsunami hits. Ships fill up with water and sink. People can drown.

41 What was the worst tsunami in United States history?

An Alaskan earthquake on March 27, 1964, created a giant tsunami that wrecked the coasts of Canada, Washington, Oregon, and California, and killed 11 people. But the most damaging one was the 1946 Alaskan tsunami that killed 165 people in Alaska and Hawaii.

42 What were the worst tsunamis ever?

The 1883 explosion on the island of Krakatoa in the Pacific Ocean generated 135-foot waves. The waves even reached Europe on the other side of the earth! The December 26, 2004, Indian Ocean earthquake triggered a series of tsunamis that killed more than 225,000 people in 11 countries, including Indonesia, Sri Lanka, India, and Thailand. It was one of the deadliest natural disasters in history.

AVALANCHES

43 What is an avalanche?

Avalanches are sudden downward movements of snow, ice, rocks, or a mixture of all of these things. Usually this happens very quickly. But sometimes the downward movement is slow. This movement is called creep. A landslide is a type of avalanche that involves rocks and soil.

(44) What causes a landslide?

Earthquakes can cause rock avalanches. So can sudden drops in temperature. Rain and melting snow collect in the cracks on a mountainside. Water can freeze, expand, and shatter the rocks when the temperature drops. The loose rocks tumble downward, picking up speed and other rocks.

(45) What damage does a landslide cause?

The worst rock avalanche in North America took place on April 29, 1903, on Turtle Mountain in Alberta, Canada. Ninety million tons of rock tumbled down the mountain at 60 miles per hour. The rockslide killed 70 people.

(46) What causes a snow avalanche?

Snow avalanches begin when a mass of snow the size of a house breaks away from a mountainside and tumbles downhill. The avalanche picks up speed and grows larger like a huge snowball. Snow avalanches have reached speeds of over 200 miles per hour.

47 How often do snow avalanches happen?

About 100,000 snow avalanches occur in the western United States and Canada every winter. Each year a dozen or more people die in snow avalanches.

48 What causes a mudslide?

Mudslides happen when there is a lot of rain on steep hills or mountains. Slopes without trees or plants often have mudslides during and after very heavy rains. The water-saturated ground can begin to slide downhill.

49 What is an underwater landslide?

Earthquakes sometimes trigger underwater landslides. Landslides move much faster in water than in air. Underwater landslides can reach speeds of over 60 miles per hour—as fast as a speeding car—even in places where the seabed is as flat as a pancake. More than 2,000 people died after a 1998 earthquake in New Guinea because a giant undersea landslide caused a huge tsunami.

(50) Can we predict avala...

Scientists can tell when the risk of an avalanche
increases. However, they are not yet able to pred
where or when an avalanche will occur.

INDEX